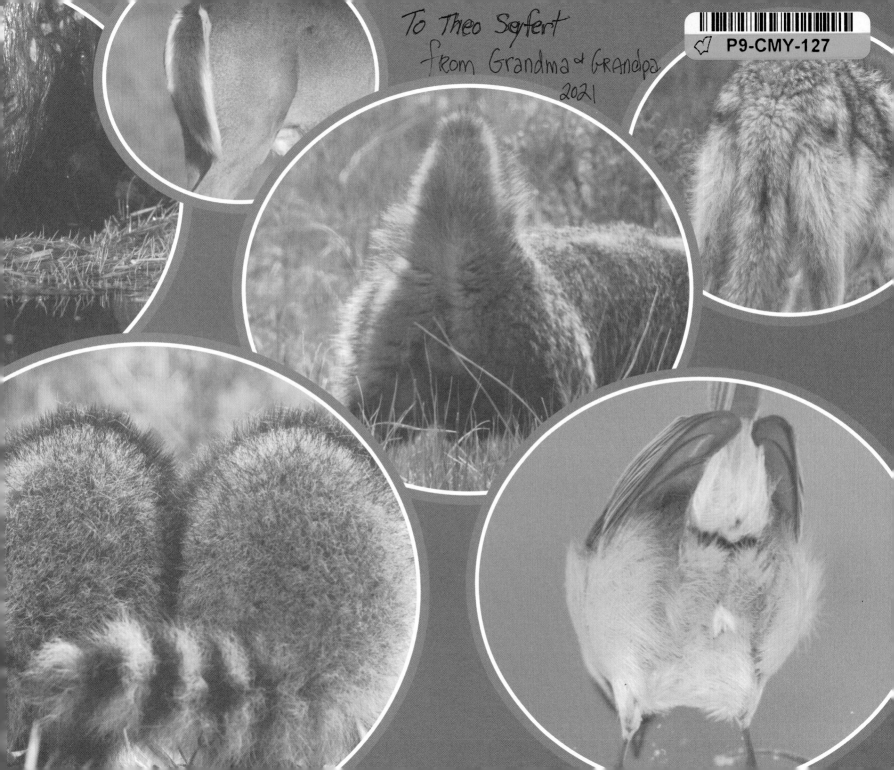

To Theo Seyfert
from Grandma & Grandpa
2021

Whose BUTT?

by Stan Tekiela

Adventure Publications
Cambridge, Minnesota

Dedication

Dedicated to my daughter, Abby. My love for you is greater than the entire outdoors.

All photos by Stan Tekiela

Cover and book design by Jonathan Norberg

20 19 18 17 16 15 14

Whose Butt?

Published by Adventure Publications
An imprint of AdventureKEEN
310 Garfield Street South
Cambridge, Minnesota 55008
(800) 678-7006
www.adventurepublications.net
Printed in China
ISBN 978-1-59193-374-8 (pbk.); ISBN 978-1-59193-444-8 (ebook)

It's the Photographer!

I love taking pictures of animals, but it's not always easy. Sometimes the animals run or fly away. When this happens, I only get pictures of their butts . . .

. . . but can you name the animals I tried to take pictures of?

This may look like an ordinary animal butt . . .

. . . but watch what happens when it dashes away.

Whose butt is this?

It's a  Deer!

When a white-tailed deer senses danger, its tail shoots up in the air. **BOING!** The white on the underside of a deer's tail is like a warning flag. It tells other deer that danger is near, so **run, run away quick!**

With a long shaggy tail,
it looks like a dog's butt . . .

. . . but you wouldn't want
to pet this behind.

Whose butt is this?

It's a Wolf!

A gray wolf can communicate with its tail. To tell other wolves that it's the leader of the pack, a wolf holds its tail up high. A frightened wolf puts its tail between its legs. An excited wolf might wag its tail.

There's a funny shaped tail on this butt . . .

. . . but you'll be surprised what a flat tail can do.

Whose butt is this?

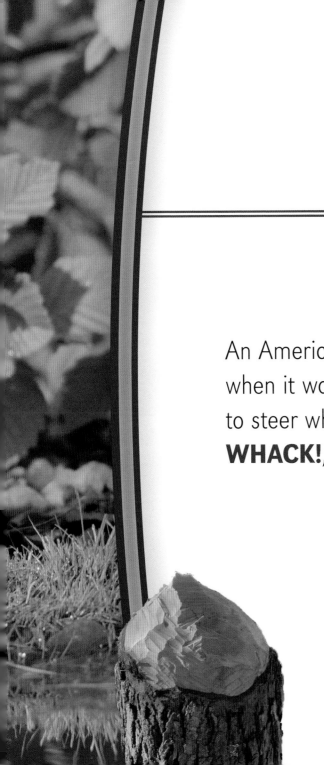

It's a Beaver!

An American beaver has a wide, flat tail that makes it waddle when it walks. But its tail is very helpful. A beaver uses its tail to steer while swimming. Also, one slap of its tail on the water, **WHACK!**, will let other beavers know that danger is near.

It's white and fluffy like a bunny's butt . . .

. . . but this rump can run incredibly fast.

Whose butt is this?

It's a Pronghorn!

Pronghorns are the fastest land mammals in North America. They can zip across the prairie at 70 miles per hour. That's as fast as a car. **VAROOM!** If you glimpse one of these speedsters, you may only see its fluffy white behind as it races away.

This critter raised
the tail on its butt . . .

. . . but don't get
close to find out why.

Whose butt is this?

It's a Skunk!

A striped skunk has a stinky way of protecting itself. When it feels threatened, a skunk will spin around and raise its tail. Other animals had better stay away, or they'll get sprayed. A skunk shoots a smelly, oily substance out of its rear. **PHEW!**

This critter may have a cute, fuzzy butt . . .

. . . but it's part of a powerful digging machine.

Whose butt is this?

It's a Badger!

Growly and snarly American badgers have short, powerful legs. Their bodies are built for burrowing. When they dig a hole, you'll quickly see their rumps disappearing behind a pile of dirt. Badgers spend more time underground than above.

This animal likes to show off its butt . . .

. . . but there's a reason it shakes its tail feathers.

Whose butt is this?

It's a Grouse!

Dusky grouse have plain-looking tail feathers. But when they fan out their tails . . . **WOW!** A boy grouse struts about and dances. He shakes his tail feathers to show off for the girl grouse.

That sure is a large
and fuzzy butt . . .

. . . but all that fur is useful
when it's cold!

Whose butt is this?

It's a Bear!

A black bear is covered in fur from its head to its rump. A bear's soft underfur keeps it warm during cold months. Its rough outer fur protects the bear from bug bites. A bear's fur also repels water. After a dunk in a river, a bear shakes like a dog to dry off.

These animals have striped tails on their butts . . .

. . . but what are these critters looking for?

Whose butts are these?

They're Raccoons!

Northern raccoons are nocturnal, meaning they come out mostly at night. They have dark masks across their faces and dark rings around their tails. These markings help them hide in the shadows at night as they look for food.

This tiny critter has a twitchy butt . . .

. . . but there's a reason it flutters about.

Whose butt is this?

It's a Chickadee!

Black-capped chickadees' twitchy tails help them dart about as they feed. During winter, small birds, like chickadees, struggle to stay warm. So they need to be quick when searching for food. **ZIP!** Food gives them the energy to stay warm.

Animal Facts

White-tailed Deer

Male deer are called bucks. They grow antlers each spring. Their antlers fall off in the winter.

Female deer are called does. They don't grow antlers.

Baby deer are called fawns. They are covered with white spots to help them blend into the forest.

Gray Wolf

Wolves live in family groups called packs. A pack can include a mother and a father, aunts and uncles, and several pups.

Everyone in a pack helps feed the pups and keep them safe.

Packs usually have six to seven members. But some packs can have up to 30 wolves.

American Beaver

Beavers have sharp upper front teeth called incisors. They use these teeth to cut down small trees.

Beavers are master builders. They use branches to construct dams and lodges.

Beavers are the largest native members of the rodent family in North America.

Pronghorn

Pronghorns are so fast they can outrun coyotes, wolves and other predators. Pronghorns can run at full speed for nearly a mile.

Both males and females have horns. The horns curve backward. But a small part of their horns faces forward. This part, called a prong, gives them their common name.

Striped Skunk

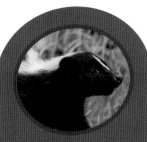

Before a skunk sprays, it stamps its feet, hisses, and raises its tail to ward off danger. But if a predator (or person) doesn't back away, then the skunk will spray a smelly, oily substance at them.

A skunk's spray smells so bad that it can stop a grizzly bear in its tracks.

American Badger

Badgers have short, powerful legs with very long claws. They are the fastest diggers in North America. In loose dirt they can dig a hole so fast that they'll disappear from sight in under two minutes.

Badgers dig large holes for dens. But they also dig to hunt their favorite food, prairie dogs.

Dusky Grouse

Grouse perform an amazing mating dance. To attract a female, male grouse will fan their tail feathers out and strut about. They'll inflate the air sacs located in their necks to impress females. They also make soft noises to call out to female grouse.

Grouse have feathers all the way down to their toes.

Black Bear

Not all black bears are actually black. They can also be brown or shades of blue. Some are even tan or pure white.

Black bears hibernate during cold winter months. They crawl into their dens and go to sleep. They'll stay in their dens until spring. Bear cubs are born in February while their mother is still in her winter den.

Northern Raccoon

Raccoons have five fingers on their hands like people do. Raccoons are also very smart and curious, and they are able to open doors and windows.

Raccoons can use their hands to catch and eat insects and frogs. They are also known for using their hands to wash their food.

Black-capped Chickadee

Chickadees are tiny, friendly birds. They are often the first birds to discover a new bird feeder in your backyard.

Chickadees enjoy singing, and they'll sing all day long. Part of their song sounds like their name, "chick-a-dee-dee-dee."

Chickadees are found in flocks that often are made up of family members.

About the Author

Naturalist, wildlife photographer and writer Stan Tekiela is the originator of the popular Wildlife and Nature Appreciation book series that includes *Bird Trivia*. has authored more than 190 educational books, including field guides, quick guides, nature books, children's books, playing cards and more, presenting many species of animals and plants.

With a Bachelor of Science degree in Natural History from the University of Minnesota and as an active professional naturalist for more than 30 years, Stan studies and photographs wildlife throughout the United States and Canada. He has received various national and regional awards for his books and photographs. Also a well-known columnist and radio personality, his syndicated column appears in more than 25 newspapers, and his wildlife programs are broadcast on a number of Midwest radio stations. Stan can be followed on Facebook and Twitter. He can be contacted via www.naturesmart.com.

More Children's Books from Stan

Stan Tekiela's books for children feature gorgeous photographs of real animals paired with captivating text. They introduce children to common, interesting and important types of North American animals.

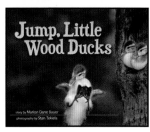